COOL
Bacon
Recipes

Main Dishes for Beginning Chefs

Alex Kuskowski

Checkerboard Library

An Imprint of Abdo Publishing
abdopublishing.com

abdopublishing.com

Published by Abdo Publishing, a division of ABDO, PO Box 398166, Minneapolis, Minnesota 55439. Copyright © 2017 by Abdo Consulting Group, Inc. International copyrights reserved in all countries. No part of this book may be reproduced in any form without written permission from the publisher. Checkerboard Library™ is a trademark and logo of Abdo Publishing.

Printed in the United States of America,
North Mankato, Minnesota
102016
012017

THIS BOOK CONTAINS
RECYCLED MATERIALS

Design and Production: Mighty Media, Inc.
Series Editor: Liz Salzmann
Photo Credits: Mighty Media, Inc.; Shutterstock

The following manufacturers/names appearing in this book are trademarks: Arm & Hammer®, Betty Crocker®, Bisquick®, Calumet®, Essential Everyday™, Kemps®, Kraft®, Maple Grove Farms of Vermont®, Oster®, Pyrex®

Publisher's Cataloging-in-Publication Data

Names: Kuskowski, Alex, author.
Title: Cool bacon recipes: main dishes for beginning chefs / by Alex Kuskowski.
Other titles: Main dishes for beginning chefs
Description: Minneapolis, MN : Abdo Publishing, 2017. | Series: Cool main dish recipes | Includes bibliographical references and index.
Identifiers: LCCN 2016944683 | ISBN 9781680781328 (lib. bdg.) | ISBN 9781680775525 (ebook)
Subjects: LCSH: Cooking--Juvenile literature. | Dinners and dining--Juvenile literature. | Entrees (Cooking)--Juvenile literature. | One-dish meals--Juvenile literature.
Classification: DDC 641.82--dc23
LC record available at http://lccn.loc.gov/2016944683

TO ADULT HELPERS

Get cooking! This is your chance to help a budding chef. Being able to cook meals is a life skill. Learning to cook gives kids new experiences and helps them gain confidence. These recipes are designed to help kids learn how to cook on their own. They may need more assistance on some recipes than others. Be there to offer guidance when they need it. Encourage them to do as much as they can on their own. Make sure to have rules for cleanup. There should always be adult supervision when kids are using sharp utensils or a hot oven or stove.

SAFETY FIRST!

Some recipes call for activities or ingredients that require caution. If you see these symbols, ask an adult for help.

HOT STUFF!
This recipe requires the use of a stove or oven. Always use pot holders when handling hot objects.

SUPER SHARP!
This recipe includes the use of a sharp utensil, such as a knife or grater.

NUT ALERT!
Some people can get very sick if they eat nuts. If you cook something with nuts, let people know!

Contents

Makin' Bacon!   4

I ♥ Bacon   6

Cooking Basics   8

Cooking Terms   10

Ingredients   12

Tools   14

Perfect Bacon Pancakes   16

Cheesy BLT Pizza   18

Bacon & Eggs All Wrapped Up   20

Tasty Wrapped Dogs   22

Eggy Bacon Pie   24

Parmesan Bacon Pasta   26

Chicken Bacon Salad   28

Conclusion   30

Glossary   31

Websites   31

Index   32

Makin' Bacon!

The main dish is where you start when planning a meal. It's the most important part. Then you choose salads, side dishes, and **desserts** to go with the main dish. Bacon is a great base for many main dishes. It is a favorite meat of people all over the world. Bacon is easy to make, tasty to eat, and there are tons of ways to prepare it!

Bacon goes with every meal. Serve it for breakfast in bacon

pancakes. Have it for lunch on a salad. Make a BLT pizza for dinner.

Try all of the bacon recipes in this book. Then think of your own ways to cook bacon. The possibilities are endless!

BAKE THAT BACON!

Check out an easy way to cook bacon!

INGREDIENTS
uncooked bacon strips

TOOLS
baking sheet
aluminum foil
pot holders
fork
paper towels

1. Preheat the oven to 400 degrees. Line the baking sheet with aluminum foil.

2. Put the bacon strips on the sheet.

3. Bake for 15 minutes or until the bacon is golden brown. Turn the strips over halfway through.

4. Place the bacon on paper towels to drain.

I ♥ BACON

Choosing the right bacon can be tough! There are many kinds available. Use this bacon guide to select the best bacon for your recipes.

KINDS OF BACON

PORK BACON is the most popular kind of bacon. It is made from pigs.

TURKEY BACON is made from turkey. It is lean and healthy.

FAKE BACON is not made from meat. But it is made to taste like bacon.

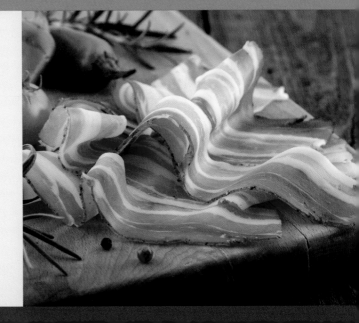

FLAVORS OF BACON

Bacon can be prepared different ways.

SMOKED BACON. Most bacon is **smoked** before it gets to the store. Smoking flavors and preserves the bacon.

CURED BACON. Most bacon is **cured**. It makes the bacon last longer.

PEPPERED BACON. Some bacon is covered with spices. When you eat it, you can taste the added seasonings.

PORK BACON CUTS

SIDE BACON comes from **pork** belly. It has long streaks of fat.

BACK BACON comes from the middle of the back. It is also called *Canadian bacon*.

....

KEEP IT CLEAN

Wash your hands before and after touching the meat. Wash any **utensils** that touched raw meat separately from other dishes.

COOKING BASICS

Ask Permission

- Before you cook, ask **permission** to use the kitchen, cooking tools, and ingredients.

- If you'd like to do something yourself, say so! Just remember to be safe.

- If you would like help, ask for it!

Be Prepared

- Be organized. Knowing where everything is makes cooking safer and more fun!

- Read the directions all the way through before starting a recipe. Follow the directions in order.

- The most important ingredient is preparation! Make sure you have everything you'll need.

Be Smart, Be Safe

- Never cook if you are home alone.

- Always have an adult nearby for hot jobs, such as using the oven or the stove.

- Have an adult around when using a sharp tool, such as a knife or a grater. Always be careful when using these tools!

- Remember to turn pot handles toward the back of the stove. That way you won't accidentally knock the pots over.

Be Neat, Be Clean

- Start with clean hands, clean tools, and a clean work surface.

- Tie back long hair to keep it out of the food.

- Wear comfortable clothing and roll up your sleeves.

- Put extra ingredients and tools away when you're done.

- Wash all the dishes and **utensils**. Clean up your workspace.

COOKING TERMS

BEAT
Beat means to mix well using a whisk or electric mixer.

DICE
Dice means to cut something into small squares.

DRAIN
Drain means to remove liquid using a colander or the pot lid.

SLICE
Slice means to cut something into pieces of the same thickness.

SPRINKLE
Sprinkle means to drop small pieces of something.

CHOP

Chop means to cut something into small pieces.

CUBE

Cube means to cut something into bite-size squares.

PEEL

Peel means to remove something's skin, often with a peeler.

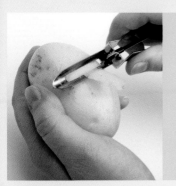

SHRED

Shred means to cut small pieces of something using a grater.

STIR

Stir means to mix ingredients together, usually with a large spoon.

WHISK

Whisk means to beat quickly by hand with a whisk or a fork.

INGREDIENTS
Here are some of the ingredients you will need.

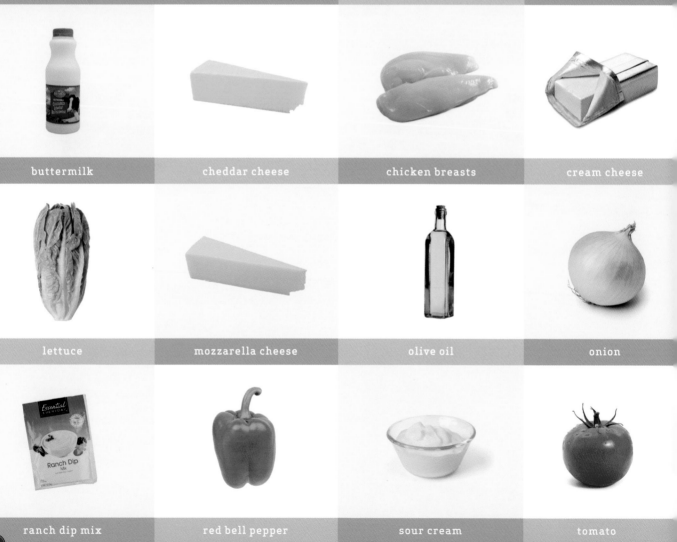

	apple-smoked bacon	bacon
buttermilk	cheddar cheese	chicken breasts	cream cheese
lettuce	mozzarella cheese	olive oil	onion
ranch dip mix	red bell pepper	sour cream	tomato

baking mix	baking powder	baking soda	bow tie pasta
dried cranberries	eggs	garlic	green onions
panko bread crumbs	Parmesan cheese, shredded	potato	pre-made pizza crust
turkey bacon	vanilla extract	vinaigrette	walnuts

13

TOOLS

Here are some of the tools you will need.

aluminum foil

baking sheet

electric frying pan

frying pan

glass pie plate

pizza pan

ramekins

rubber spatula

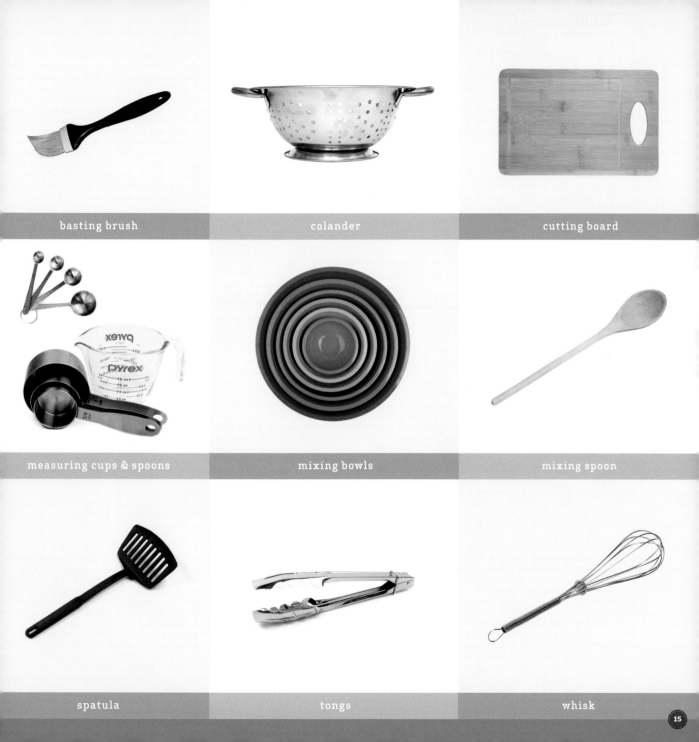

basting brush

colander

cutting board

measuring cups & spoons

mixing bowls

mixing spoon

spatula

tongs

whisk

PERFECT
Bacon Pancakes

A maple-flavored main dish for breakfast!

INGREDIENTS

2 strips bacon
¾ cup buttermilk
1 cup flour
2 tablespoons sugar
1 teaspoon baking powder
½ teaspoon baking soda
½ teaspoon salt
½ teaspoon vanilla extract

1 egg
non-stick cooking spray

TOOLS

measuring cups
measuring spoons
large mixing bowl
whisk
electric frying pan
spatula

1. Follow the steps on page 5 to bake the bacon. Break the strips in half.

2. Put the buttermilk, flour, sugar, baking powder, baking soda, salt, vanilla, and egg in the mixing bowl. Whisk the ingredients together. Pour the mixture into a glass measuring cup.

3. Coat the frying pan with non-stick spray. Set the heat to medium.

4. Pour one-fourth of the pancake mixture into the frying pan. Press a bacon strip into the batter. Cook it until the batter bubbles.

5. Flip the pancake. Cook it until both sides are golden brown.

6. Repeat steps 4 and 5 with the remaining batter.

2

4

5

CHEESY
BLT Pizza

Make a perfectly delicious pizza!

12 strips bacon
¾ cup sour cream
¼ cup mayonnaise
8 ounces cream cheese
1 package ranch dip mix
2 (16-ounce) premade
   pizza crusts

2 cups shredded
   mozzarella cheese
½ onion, chopped
2 tomatoes, diced
1 cup shredded lettuce

measuring cups
sharp knife
cutting board
large mixing bowl
mixing spoon
pizza pan
rubber spatula
pot holders

1   Follow the steps on page 5 to bake the bacon. Chop the bacon into small pieces.

2   Preheat the oven to 425 degrees. Put the sour cream, mayonnaise, cream cheese, and dip mix in a large bowl. Stir the ingredients together.

3   Put a pizza crust on the pizza pan. Spread half of the sour cream mixture over the pizza crust.

4   Sprinkle half of the cheese, onion, tomatoes, and bacon on the pizza. Bake for 10 minutes.

5   Take the pizza out of the oven. Sprinkle half of the lettuce on top.

6   Repeat steps 3 through 5 to make a second pizza.

BACON & EGGS
All Wrapped Up

Make a meal wrapped up in bacon!

INGREDIENTS

4 teaspoons butter, melted

8 strips bacon

1 **medium** potato, peeled and diced

1 cup shredded cheddar cheese

4 eggs

TOOLS

vegetable peeler
sharp knife
cutting board
measuring cups
basting brush
4 ramekins
baking sheet
pot holders

① Preheat the oven to 400 degrees. Brush the insides of four ramekins with melted butter.

② Lay two strips of bacon in a ramekin. Let the ends hang over the rim.

③ Sprinkle a layer of potatoes on the bacon. Sprinkle on a layer of cheese. Add two more layers of potatoes and cheese.

④ Crack an egg on top.

⑤ Fold the ends of the bacon over the egg.

⑥ Repeat steps 2 through 5 to fill three more ramekins. Place the ramekins on a baking sheet. Bake for 30 minutes.

3

4

5

TASTY
Wrapped Dogs

Your friends will go crazy for these dogs!

INGREDIENTS

4 hot dogs
4 slices cheddar cheese
4 strips bacon
4 hot dog buns

TOOLS

baking sheet
aluminum foil
sharp knife
cutting board
pot holders

1 Preheat the oven to 400 degrees. Cover a baking sheet with aluminum foil.

2 Make a cut along the length of each hot dog. Cut about three-fourths through the hot dogs.

3 Cut the cheese slices in half. Put two pieces in the cut of each hot dog.

4 Wrap a bacon strip around each hot dog.

5 Place the wrapped hot dogs on the baking sheet. Bake for 30 minutes, or until the bacon is **crispy**.

6 Take the hot dogs out of the oven. Let them cool slightly. Put them in the hot dog buns.

2

3

4

EGGY
Bacon Pie

Go eggs & bacon crazy!

INGREDIENTS

14 strips turkey bacon

non-stick cooking spray

1 cup shredded cheddar cheese

⅓ cup chopped green onions

¼ cup chopped red bell pepper

2 cups milk

4 eggs

1 cup baking mix

¼ teaspoon black pepper

TOOLS

measuring cups

sharp knife

cutting board

measuring spoons

10-inch glass pie plate

large mixing bowl

whisk

pot holders

1. Follow the steps on page 5 to bake the bacon. Chop the bacon into small pieces.

2. Preheat the oven to 400 degrees. Coat the pie plate with non-stick spray.

3. Sprinkle the bacon, cheese, green onions and red pepper in the pie plate.

4. Put the milk, eggs, baking mix, and black pepper in the mixing bowl. Whisk the ingredients together.

5. Pour the milk mixture into the pie plate. Bake for 35 to 40 minutes.

3

4

5

PARMESAN
Bacon Pasta

Serve up a tasty meal!

INGREDIENTS

12 strips bacon
12 ounces bow tie pasta
7 tablespoons olive oil
3 cloves garlic, minced
¼ teaspoon salt
¼ teaspoon black pepper

½ cup shredded
Parmesan cheese

TOOLS

measuring spoons
sharp knife
cutting board
measuring cups
large pot
colander
mixing spoon
pot holders
6 serving bowls

1. Follow the steps on page 5 to bake the bacon. Chop the bacon into small pieces.

2. Cook the pasta according to the directions on the package. Drain the pasta. Leave it in the colander.

3. Put the olive oil, bacon, garlic, salt, and pepper in the pot. Stir the ingredients together.

4. Put the pasta back in the pot. Stir to coat the pasta with the olive oil mixture.

5. Divide the pasta between the serving bowls. Sprinkle shredded Parmesan cheese on the pasta.

2

4

5

CHICKEN
Bacon Salad

Put a new twist on a classic!

INGREDIENTS

5 strips apple-smoked bacon

½ cup flour

1 egg, beaten

¾ cup panko bread crumbs

2 chicken breasts

2 tablespoons olive oil

8 cups chopped lettuce

1 cup cubed cheddar cheese

½ cup dried cranberries

½ cup walnuts

½ teaspoon salt

½ teaspoon black pepper

6 tablespoons vinaigrette dressing

TOOLS

measuring cups

measuring spoons

sharp knife

cutting board

3 small mixing bowls

plate

frying pan

tongs

4 salad bowls

1. Follow the steps on page 5 to bake the bacon. Chop the bacon into small pieces.

2. Put the flour in a mixing bowl. Put the beaten egg in another mixing bowl. Put the panko crumbs in the third mixing bowl.

3. Dip both sides of each chicken breast in the flour. Next dip both sides in the egg. Then dip both sides in the panko crumbs. Set the chicken on a plate.

4. Put the oil in the frying pan. Heat it on high. Fry the chicken for 2 to 4 minutes on each side. Let the chicken cool. Cut it into thin slices.

5. Divide the lettuce between the salad bowls. Add cheese, bacon, chicken, dried cranberries, walnuts, salt, and pepper to each salad. Serve with vinaigrette.

3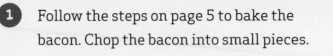

4

5

Conclusion

Explore the world of bacon dishes. What else can you cook up?

Main dishes are fun to make and share! Feel proud of the dishes you prepare. Eat them with your family and friends. Bacon is one of many great ingredients for main dishes. Don't stop with bacon. Try other ingredients too!

Glossary

crispy – hard, thin, and easy to break.

cure – to prepare meat so it won't spoil. Adding salt or sugar, cooking it, and smoking it are ways to cure meat.

dessert – a sweet food, such as fruit, ice cream, or pastry, served after a meal.

permission – when a person in charge says it's okay to do something.

pork – meat that comes from a pig.

smoke – to use smoke to give foods flavor and keep them from spoiling.

utensil – a tool used to prepare or eat food.

WEBSITES

To learn more about Cool Main Dishes, visit **booklinks.abdopublishing.com**. These links are routinely monitored and updated to provide the most current information available.

Index

A

adult help, need for, 2, 8, 9

B

bacon
    how to bake, 5
    types of, 6, 7
    use in main dishes, 4, 5, 30

C

cleanliness, guidelines for, 7, 9
creativity, in cooking, 5, 30

E

eggs, recipes for, 20, 21, 24, 25

F

friends and family, 22, 30

H

hot dogs, recipe for, 22, 23

I

ingredients
    preparation of, 8, 10, 11
    types of, 12, 13

K

kitchen use, permission for, 8

M

main dishes, definition of, 4, 5
meal planning, 4

N

nuts, allergies to, 2

P

pancakes, recipe for, 16, 17
pasta, recipe for, 26, 27
pie, recipe for, 24, 25
pizza, recipe for, 18, 19
preparation, for cooking, 8

R

recipes
    reading and following, 8
    symbols in, 2

S

safety, guidelines for, 2, 8, 9
salad, recipe for, 28, 29
sharp utensils, safe use of, 2, 9
stove and oven, safe use of, 2, 9

T

terms, about cooking, 10, 11
tools and equipment, for
        cooking, 14, 15

W

websites, about cooking main
        dishes, 31